Classic Borders

Julie Collins

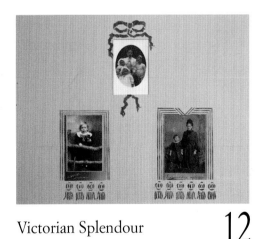

Ancient Mosaic Designs — 8

Victorian Splendour — 12

Greek Key & Crenellation — 16

Regal Swans & Scallops — 20

Fleur-de-Lys with Scrolls — 24

Roman Emperor & Columns — 28

INTRODUCING STENCILLING

Once you begin stencilling you will be amazed at the wonderful results you can obtain quite easily and without spending a great deal of money. This book introduces six themed projects and provides ready-to-use stencils that can be used with numerous variations in design – just follow the step-by-step features and simple instructions. With very little paint and only a few pieces of equipment you can achieve stunning results. Have fun!

BASIC MATERIALS

Paints and Decorative Finishes
Emulsion paint
Water-based stencil paint
Oil sticks
Acrylic paints (bottles and tubes)
Specialist paints (for fabrics, ceramics, glass etc)
Spray paints
Metallic acrylic artists' colours (gold, silver etc)
Silver and gold art flow pens
Bronze powders (various metallics)
Gilt wax

Brushes and Applicators
Art brushes (variety of sizes)
Stencil brushes (small, medium and large)
Sponge applicators
Mini-roller and tray

Other Equipment
Set square
Blotting paper
Scissors or scalpel (or craft knife)
Roll of lining paper (for practising)
Eraser
Soft pencil
Fine-tip permanent pen
Chalk or Chalkline and powdered chalk
Long rigid ruler
Tape measure
Plumbline
Spirit level
Low-tack masking tape
Spray adhesive
Tracing paper
Paint dishes or palettes
Cloths
Kitchen roll
White spirit
Stencil plastic or card
Cotton buds
Methylated spirits

CUTTING OUT STENCILS
The stencils at the back of the book are all designed to use separately or together to create many different pattern combinations. Cut along the dotted lines of the individual stencils and make sure you transfer the reference code onto each one with a permanent pen. Carefully remove the cut-out pieces of the stencil. Apply 50 mm (2 in) strips of tracing paper around the edges using masking tape; this will help to prevent smudging paint onto your surface.

REPAIRING STENCILS
Stencils may become damaged and torn from mishandling, or if the cutouts have not been removed carefully, but they are easy to repair. Keeping the stencil perfectly flat, cover both sides of the tear with masking tape. Then carefully remove any excess tape with a scalpel.

GETTING STARTED

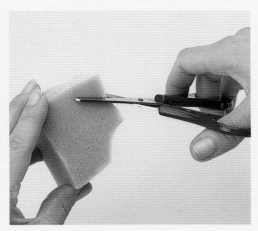

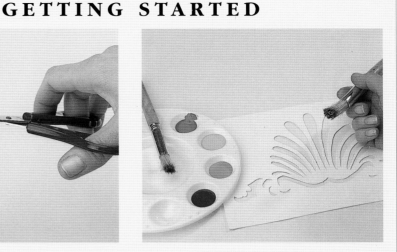

DUPLICATING STENCILS

Stencil plastic (Mylar) can be used; or card wiped over with linseed oil, which left to dry will harden and make the surface waterproof. Place the cut-out stencil on top. Trace around carefully with a permanent pen inside the cut-out shapes. Cut along the lines with a scalpel and remove the pieces. You may prefer to trace on top of the design, then transfer your tracing onto card.

MAKING A SPONGE APPLICATOR

Sponging your stencil is one of the easiest methods, but you may prefer to use a stencil brush, especially for fine detail. Using a piece of upholstery foam or very dense bath sponge, cut pieces 12–50 mm ($\frac{1}{2}$–2 in) wide and approximately 50 mm (2 in) long. Hold the four corners together and secure with tape to form a pad. You can also round off the ends with scissors or a scalpel and trim to a smooth finish. The small-ended applicators can be used for tiny, intricate patterns.

HOW TO USE WATER-BASED PAINT

Water-based paints are easy and economical to use and have the advantage of drying quickly. For professional-looking stencils, do not load your sponge or brush too heavily or you will not achieve a soft, shaded finish. Paint that is too watery will seep under the stencil edges and smudge. If the paint is too heavy you will obtain a heavy block effect rather than the soft stippling you require.

LOOKING AFTER STENCILS

Stencils have a long life if cared for correctly. Before cleaning make sure you remove any tape or tracing paper that has been added. Remove any excess paint before it dries, and wipe the stencil with a damp cloth every time you use it. If water or acrylic paint has dried and hardened, soften it with water and ease it off gently with a scalpel. Then use a small amount of methylated spirits on a cloth to remove the rest. An oil-based paint can simply be removed by wiping over the stencil with white spirit on a cloth. Stencils should be dried thoroughly before storing flat between sheets of greaseproof paper.

HOW TO USE OIL STICKS

Oil sticks may seem expensive, but in fact go a long way. They take longer to dry, allowing you to blend colours very effectively. Oil sticks are applied with a stencil brush and you need to have a different brush for each colour. Break the seal as instructed on the stick and rub a patch of the colour onto a palette, allowing space to blend colours. As the stencil sticks dry slowly, you need to lift the stencil off cleanly, and replace to continue the pattern.

PRACTISING PAINTING STENCILS

Roll out some lining paper onto a table and select the stencil you wish to practise with. Using spray adhesive, lightly spray the back of your stencil and place it into position on the paper. Prepare your paint on a palette. Dab your sponge or brush into the paint and offload excess paint onto scrap paper. Apply colour over the stencil in a light coat to create an even stippled effect. You can always stencil on a little more paint if a stronger effect is needed, but if you over apply it in the first place it is very difficult to remove. Keep separate sponges for different colours.

PLANNING YOUR DESIGN

Befure starting to stencil take time to plan your design. Decide where you want to use the patterns, then work out how to position the stencils so that the design will fit around obstacles such as doorways and corners. The techniques shown here will help you to undertake the job with a systematic approach.

PUTTING PATTERN PIECES TOGETHER

1 Before you apply your design, stencil a sample onto lining paper. Mark the centre and baseline of the design on the paper and put together your pattern pieces. You can then work out the size of the design, how it will fit into the space available and the distance required between repeats.

2 You can avoid stencilling around a corner by working out the number of pattern repeats needed, and allowing extra space either between repeats or within the pattern. Creating vertical lines through the pattern will allow you to stretch it evenly.

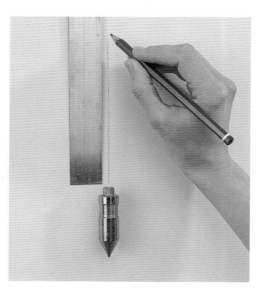

MARKING BASELINES AND HORIZONTAL LINES

Select your stencil area, and take a measure from the ceiling, doorframe, window or edging, bearing in mind the depth of your stencil. Using a spirit level, mark out a horizontal line. You can then extend this by using a chalkline or long ruler with chalk or soft pencil.

MARKING VERTICAL LINES

If you need to work out the vertical position for a stencil, hang a plumbline above the stencilling area and use a ruler to draw a vertical line with chalk or a soft pencil. You will need to use this method when creating an all-over wallpaper design.

FIXING THE STENCIL INTO PLACE

Lightly spray the back of the stencil with spray adhesive, then put it in position and smooth it down carefully. You can use low-tack masking tape if you prefer, but take care not to damage the surface to be stencilled; keep the whole stencil flat to prevent paint seeping underneath.

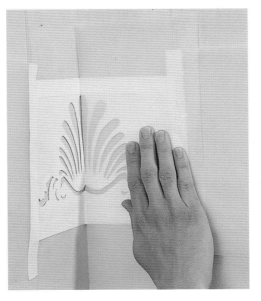

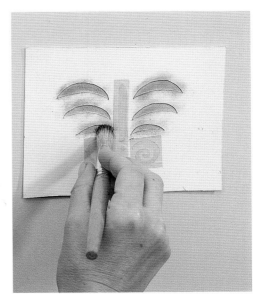

MARKING THE STENCIL FOR A PATTERN REPEAT

Attach a border of tracing paper to each edge of the stencil. Position the next pattern and overlap the tracing paper onto the previous design, tracing over the edge of it. By matching the tracing with the previous pattern as you work along you will be able to align and repeat the stencil at the same intervals.

COPING WITH CORNERS

Stencil around corners after you have finished the rest of the design, having measured to leave the correct space for the corner pattern before you do so. Then bend the stencil into the corner and mask off one side of it. Stencil the open side and allow the paint to dry, then mask off this half and stencil the other part to complete the design.

MASKING OFF PART OF A STENCIL

Use low-tack masking tape to mask out small or intricate areas of stencil. You can also use ordinary masking tape, but remove excess stickiness first by peeling it on and off your skin or a cloth once or twice. To block off inside shapes and large areas, cut out pieces of tracing paper to the appropriate size and fix them on top with spray adhesive.

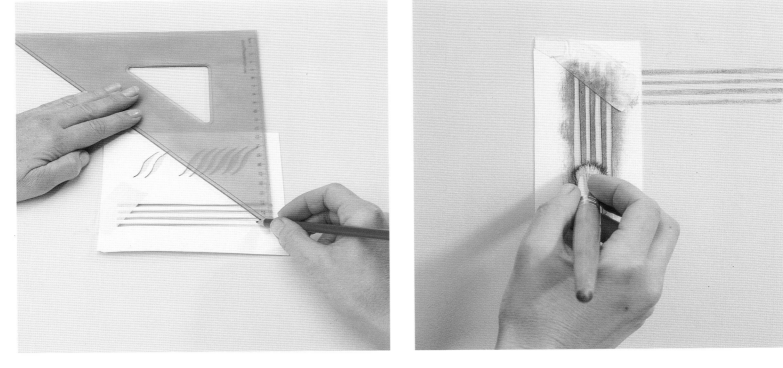

MITRING STENCIL PATTERNS

1 When you are stencilling a continuous pattern and need to make a corner, mask off the stencil by marking a 45-degree angle at both ends of the stencil with a permanent pen. Mask along this line with a piece of masking tape or tracing paper.

2 Make sure the baselines of the stencil on both sides of the corner are the same distance from the edge, and that they cross at the corner. Put the diagonal end of the stencil right into the corner and apply the paint. Turn the stencil sideways to align the other diagonal end of the stencil and turn the corner.

PAINT EFFECTS

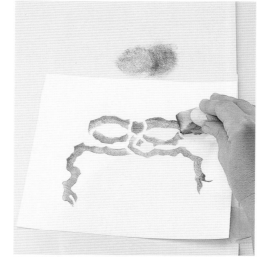

CHOOSING COLOURS

Take care to choose appropriate colours to create the effect you want. Stencil a practice piece onto paper and try a variation of colours to ensure you are pleased with the result. Different colours can make a design look entirely different. Use spray adhesive to fix your practice paper onto the surface on which you wish to produce the design so that you can assess its effect before applying the stencil.

APPLYING WATER-BASED COLOURS

Water-based paint dries quickly, so it tends to layer rather than blend. It is best applied by using a swirling movement or gently dabbing, depending on the finished effect you wish to create. Once you have applied a light base colour, you can add a darker edge for shading. Alternatively, leave some of the stencil bare and add a different tone to that area to obtain a shaded or highlighted appearance.

BLENDING OIL-STICK COLOURS

Oil sticks mix together smoothly and are perfect for blending colours. Place the colours separately on your palette and mix them with white to obtain a variety of tones or blend them together to create new colours. You can also blend by applying one coat into another with a stippling motion while stencilling. Blending looks most effective when applying a pale base coat, then shading on top with a darker colour.

HIGHLIGHTING

A simple way to add highlighting to your design is first to paint in your stencil in a light tone of your main colour, then carefully lift the stencil and move it down a fraction. Then stencil in a darker shade; this leaves the highlighted areas around the top edges of the pattern.

GILDING

After painting your stencil use gold to highlight the edges. Load a fine art brush with gold acrylic paint and carefully outline the top edges of the pattern. Use one quick brush stroke for each pattern repeat, keeping in the same direction. Other methods are to blow bronze powder onto the wet paint, draw around the pattern with a gold flow pen, or smudge on gilt wax cream, then buff to a high sheen.

APPLYING SPRAY PAINTS

Spray paints are ideal on glass, wood, metal, plastic and ceramic surfaces. They are quick to apply and fast drying, but cannot be blended, although you can achieve subtle shaded effects. Apply the paint in several thin coats. Mask off a large area around the design to protect it from the spray, which tends to drift. Try to use sprays out of doors or in a well-ventilated area. Some spray paints are non-toxic, making them ideal for children's furniture.

DIFFERENT SURFACES

BARE WOOD

Rub the wood surface down to a smooth finish. Then fix the stencil in place and paint with a thin base coat of white, so that the stencil colours will stand out well when applied. Leave the stencil in place and allow to dry thoroughly, then apply your stencil colours in the normal way. When completely dry you can apply a coat of light wax or varnish to protect your stencil.

STAINED WOOD

If you are staining wood or medium-density fibreboard (MDF) prior to stencilling, you have a choice of many different wood shades as well as a wide range of colours. If the base coat is dark, stencil a thin coat of white paint on top. Apply your stencil and protect with a coat of clear varnish when it is completely dry.

FABRIC

Use special fabric paint for stencilling on fabric and follow the manufacturer's instructions carefully. Place card or blotting paper behind the fabric while working and keep the material taut. If you are painting a dark fabric, best results are achieved by stencilling first with white or a lighter shade. Heat seal the design following the manufacturer's instructions.

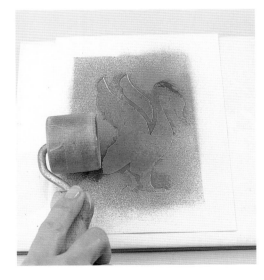

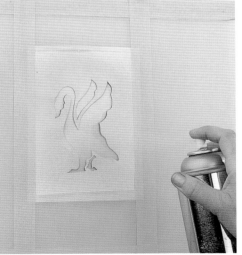

CERAMICS

Use special ceramic paints to work directly onto glazed ceramic tiles, and unglazed ceramics such as terracotta. Make sure all surfaces are clean, so that the stencils can be fixed easily. Apply the paint with a brush, sponge, spray or mini-roller. Ceramic paints are durable and washable, and full manufacturer's instructions are given on the container.

GLASS

Before applying the stencil make sure the glass is clean, spray on a light coat of adhesive and place the stencil in position. Spray on water-based or ceramic paint, remove the stencil and allow to dry. If you wish to stencil drinking glasses, use special non-toxic and water-resistant glass paints. An etched-glass look with stencils on windows, doors and mirrors can be achieved with a variety of materials.

PAINTED SURFACES

Stencils can be applied to surfaces painted with matt, satin or vinyl silk emulsion, oil scumble glazes, acrylic glazes and varnishes, and to matt wallpaper. If you wish to decorate a gloss surface, stencil first with an acrylic primer, leave to dry and then stencil the colours on top. Surfaces to be stencilled need to be smooth so that the stencil can lay flat.

ANCIENT MOSAIC DESIGNS

The mosaics in this design are perfect to decorate a bathroom, table top, garden wall, small plant pots or trays. The possibilities are endless and other projects could include creating a mosaic effect on a plain wooden or concrete floor. The wave and flower motifs can be used separately to make a decorative border or corner as well as being part of a mosaic pattern. Use bright, vibrant colours to turn a plain surface into a striking masterpiece.

PAINT COLOUR GUIDE

Purple   Emerald green

Fuchsia pink Electric blue

CREATING THE TILED EFFECT

1 Work out the position of stencil A by starting in the middle of the straight edge, leaving spaces or infilling with parts of the stencil as necessary.

2 When you reach the corners, do not turn the stencil, but simply move it along the side border as shown in the photograph below.

3 Stencil C can be positioned as a centrepiece or used as an alternative all-over pattern.

PROJECT PATTERN

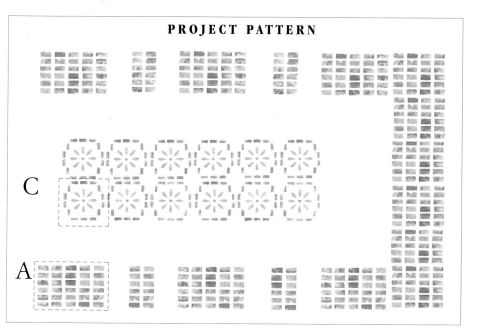

CREATING MULTI-COLOURED MOSAICS
Position stencil A and apply small pieces of low-tack masking tape, leaving only a few tiles exposed. Apply the first colour with a sponge applicator. When dry, reposition the tape to cover the painted areas and apply a different colour with a new applicator, and continue in this way until all the tile area is complete.

INFILLING THE MOSAIC PATTERN
By using the plain mosaic tile stencil A, you can mask off any areas to infill spaces between patterns. To create the side borders, vertically align three or four tile widths (masking off the others) and continue to stencil vertically along the border.

WAVE VARIATION BORDER
Align wave stencil B along the edge of your mosiac border (stencil A). Create a dramatic ocean effect by blending electric blue and emerald green paint, highlighting the top of the wave in green and the bottom of it in blue.

ANCIENT MOSAIC DESIGNS VARIATIONS

These are just a few of the designs that you can create for original mosaic floors, tiles and borders. Use vibrant shades of electric blue and emerald green or rich earth colours such as siennas, ochres and umbers. Combining the stencil patterns will give you greater flexibility with your designs, but you can also replicate an ancient tiled floor effect by just using the flower motif C.

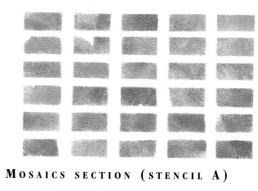

MOSAICS SECTION (STENCIL A)

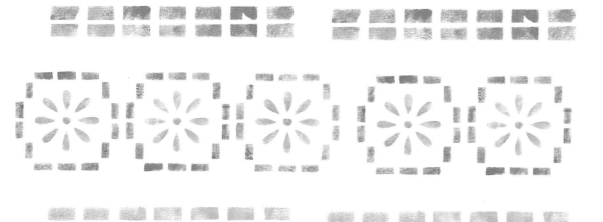

MOSAICS AND WAVE BORDER (STENCILS A AND B)

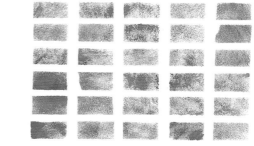

FLOWERS AND MOSAIC (STENCIL C)

MOSAICS AND FLOWERS BAND (STENCILS A AND C)

BLOCK MOSAICS REPEAT (STENCIL A)

WAVES EDGING (STENCIL B)

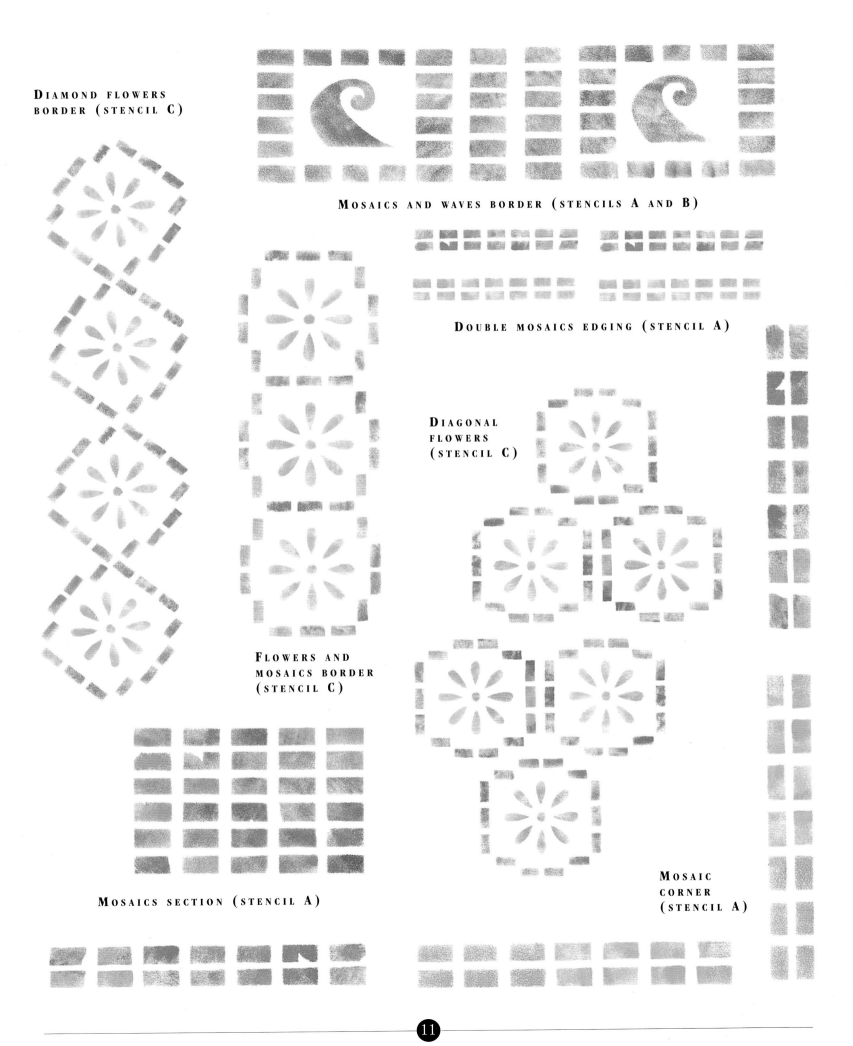

DIAMOND FLOWERS BORDER (STENCIL C)

MOSAICS AND WAVES BORDER (STENCILS A AND B)

DOUBLE MOSAICS EDGING (STENCIL A)

DIAGONAL FLOWERS (STENCIL C)

FLOWERS AND MOSAICS BORDER (STENCIL C)

MOSAICS SECTION (STENCIL A)

MOSAIC CORNER (STENCIL A)

VICTORIAN SPLENDOUR

The Victorian love of opulence was the inspiration for these designs of swags, tails, tassels and bows. I have painted them in period colours of dark red and green against a neutral background, and they could also be decorated with gold leaf. The stencils can be used to make borders and picture frames and to enhance a display of family photographs. Or you could transform a plain photograph album into a beautiful personalized gift by stencilling borders and decorative photograph mounts.

PAINT COLOUR GUIDE

Burgundy red   Dark green   Gold

A Victorian Photo Display

1 Take a 12.5 x 10 cm (5 x 4 in) print and place it centre top, then place bow stencil A above and around it. Separate the bow ribbons to trail down underneath the print.

2 Fix two lower prints into position with spray adhesive as shown and position stencil C around the edges of the prints to form a frame. Using stencil D, apply a row of tassels under each print.

3 Fix two wider prints to make the bottom row. You can create frames by using stencil C, or stencil a row of swags and tassels along the bottom edge by using stencils B and D.

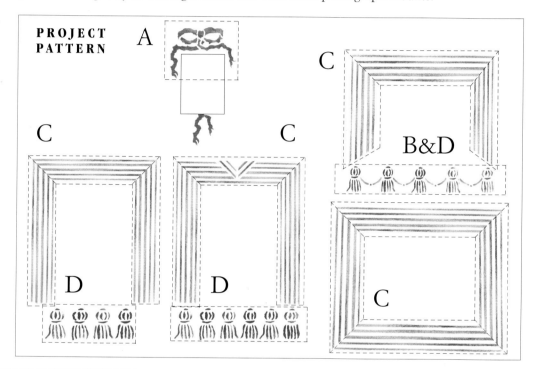

PROJECT PATTERN

A

C

C

C

C

B&D

D

D

C

APPLYING THE PAINT
Using water-based stencil paint, dip a stencil brush into the paint, then wipe the excess off onto a cloth. Stipple the paint into the stencil shapes with an up and down stabbing motion. For the bows use a gentle circular motion.

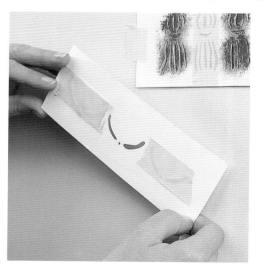

COMBINING THE COLOURS
Take stencils B and D and mask off every alternate tassel and the outside swags – the two stencils will fit perfectly together and make swags and tails. Use dark red paint for stencil D and dark green for stencil B.

CREATING THE PRINTS
Make sepia prints by laser-copying old photographs. Spray the surface with artists' fixing spray to prevent colour run, then paste into position.

A.SWANLUND NORTH FINCHLEY.

Emberson & Sons

G WILTON ROAD
BELGRAVIA & CHERTSEY.
S.W. SURREY.

VICTORIAN SPLENDOUR VARIATIONS

These stencils can be used to create beautiful wall borders, friezes and ornate pelmets. Pastel or dramatic colours look most effective and a very pretty decoration can be obtained by stencilling pale blue or pink bows or tassels. You can also create a sumptuous antique look by stencilling with gold sticks or gilt cream on picture frames. Similarly, you can use the designs as decoration on furniture.

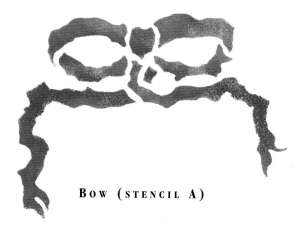

FRAME AND TASSELS (STENCILS C AND D)

TASSELS AND SWAGS (STENCILS B AND D)

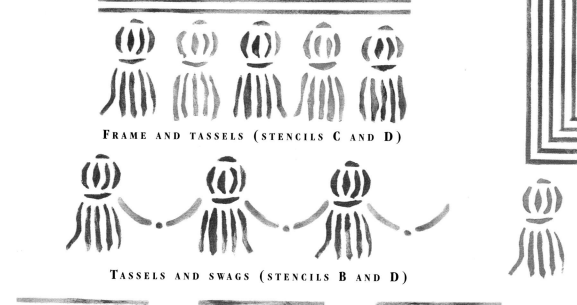

BOW, FRAME AND TASSELS (STENCILS A, C AND D)

FRAME AND SWAGS (STENCILS B AND C)

BOW (STENCIL A)

LONG SWAGS AND TASSELS (STENCILS B AND D)

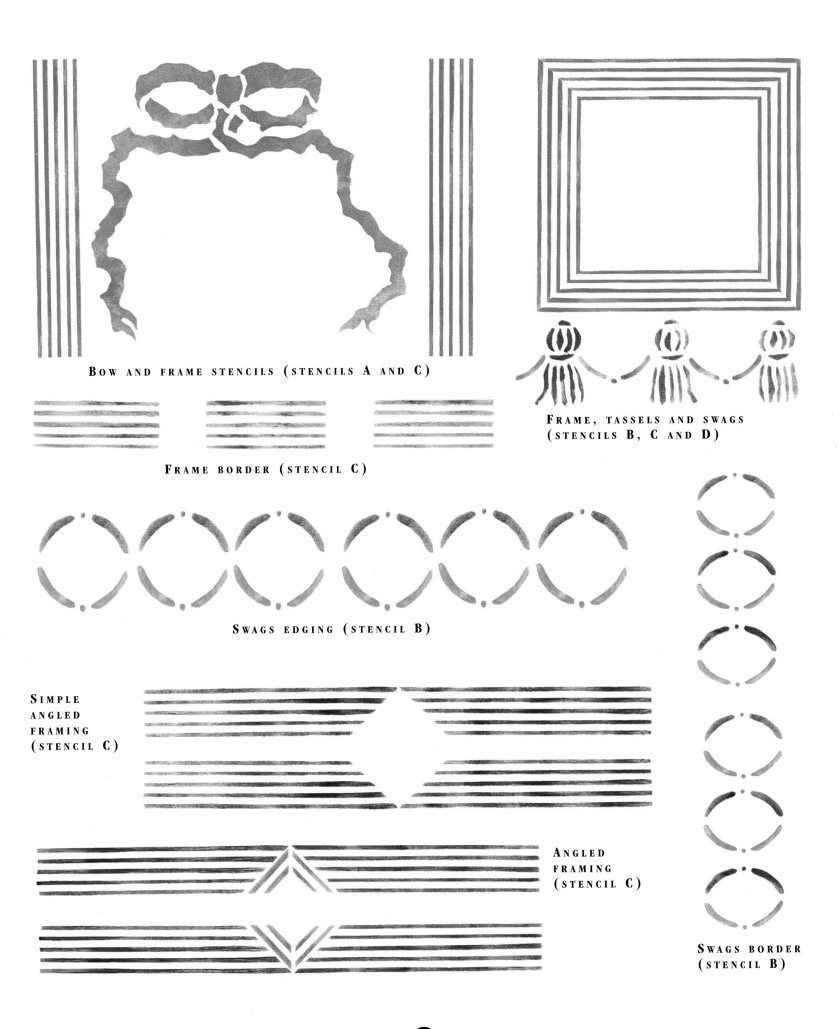

BOW AND FRAME STENCILS (STENCILS A AND C)

FRAME, TASSELS AND SWAGS (STENCILS B, C AND D)

FRAME BORDER (STENCIL C)

SWAGS EDGING (STENCIL B)

SIMPLE ANGLED FRAMING (STENCIL C)

ANGLED FRAMING (STENCIL C)

SWAGS BORDER (STENCIL B)

GREEK KEY & CRENELLATION

Similar designs to these have been used to enhance the architectural features of buildings since 421BC. Stencil B is based on a traditional design that bears the descriptive name Erechtheion, in reference to the Ancient Greek temple on the Acropolis in Athens. It can be used effectively to design your own personalized wallpaper. With the Greek key stencil C you can create a wonderful three-dimensional effect by using toned colours and simple highlighting. Use the crenellation stencil A to stencil under any plain coving to give the appearance of a carved or moulded architrave.

PAINT COLOUR GUIDE

Pewter metallic   Grey   Silver

POSITIONING GREEK KEY CORNERS

1 Two special corner pieces have been designed so that you can turn a corner at a 90-degree angle and still keep the continuity of the pattern of the Greek key stencil C when using it for a border or frame or on a floor.

2 Each complete run of the pattern starts off with stencil D, continues with repeats of stencil C, and ends with stencil E. Thus stencil D is in the left-hand corner, and stencil E in the right-hand corner on a straight run.

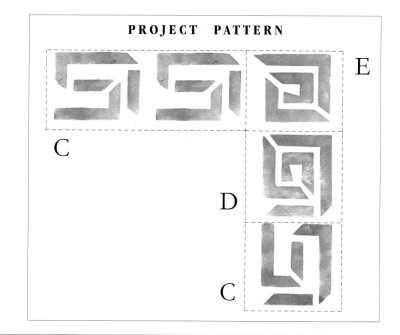

PROJECT PATTERN

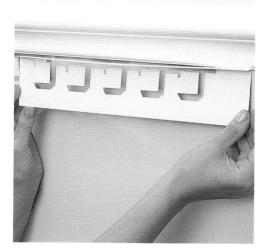

POSITIONING THE STENCIL UNDER AN ARCHITRAVE
In order to stencil the design directly below the coving, fold forward the excess stencil card along the dotted line. This will enable you to slot the stencil directly under the coving in the correct position and prevent smudging.

CRENELLATION AS AN ARCHITRAVE
Position the stencil directly under the coving or moulding using spray adhesive. To avoid the pattern looking too bold, mix some white acrylic paint into the pewter colour and apply a thin coat of paint with gentle circular motions.

HIGHLIGHTING
Imagine a ray of light striking the top edges of the pattern. Draw this highlighting with a silver flow art pen, or paint on a fine line of highlighter with an art brush. Use a ruler to paint the straight edges.

GREEK KEY & CRENELLATION VARIATIONS

I have used silver and pewter tones in my project, but other colours such as black, white, gold and Venetian red can be used to give dramatic effect on various background shades on fabrics, furniture and murals. You can create a marbled effect by stencilling with grey or black, then lightly brush across with a white artists' paint to achieve a classic look.

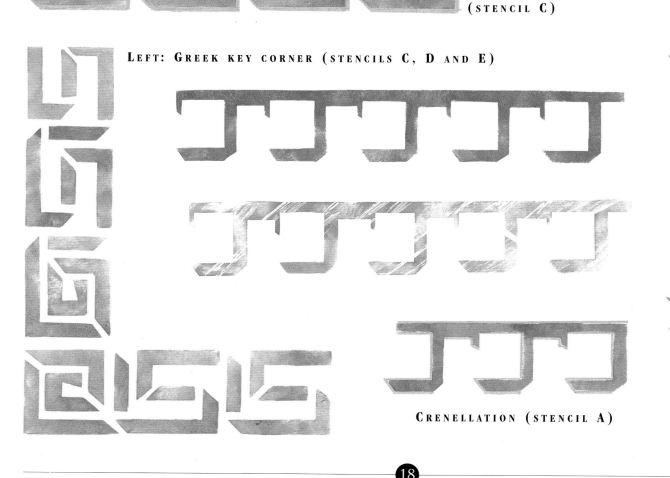

GREEK KEY MOTIFS (STENCILS D AND E)

GREEK KEY BORDER (STENCILS C, D AND E)

LEFT: GREEK KEY BORDER (STENCIL C)

RIGHT: ERECHTHEION DROP (STENCIL B)

LEFT: GREEK KEY CORNER (STENCILS C, D AND E)

CRENELLATION (STENCIL A)

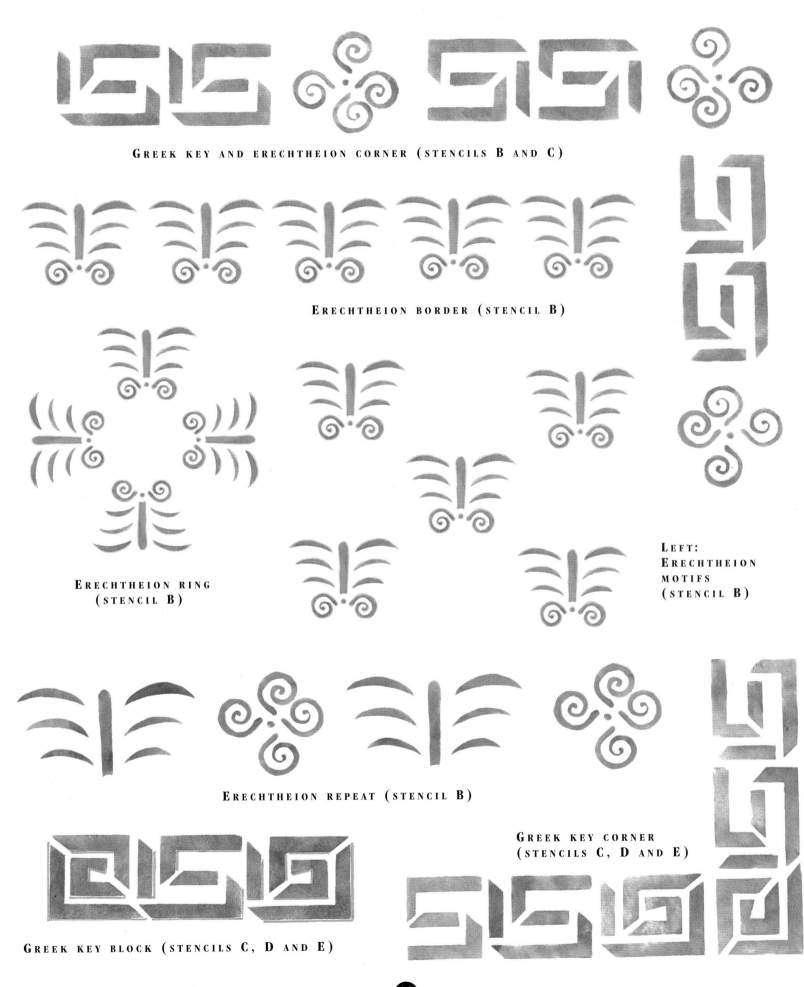

GREEK KEY AND ERECHTHEION CORNER (STENCILS B AND C)

ERECHTHEION BORDER (STENCIL B)

ERECHTHEION RING
(STENCIL B)

LEFT:
ERECHTHEION
MOTIFS
(STENCIL B)

ERECHTHEION REPEAT (STENCIL B)

GREEK KEY CORNER
(STENCILS C, D AND E)

GREEK KEY BLOCK (STENCILS C, D AND E)

REGAL SWANS & SCALLOPS

Cool jade and aqua colours give a feeling of fountains, old urns and spring freshness, and will enhance any bathroom, kitchen or garden wall. The effect here is achieved by blending deep jade and white stencil oil sticks together. Scallop and bird designs date back to Ancient Greece, and these versatile motifs can be combined in many different ways. All three parts of the stencil can also be used individually; the scallop design looks particularly attractive on plain walls or lining paper.

PAINT COLOUR GUIDE

Bright jade   White   Gold

POSITIONING THE STENCILS

1 Mark out a horizontal line on the wall, then position the scallop stencil C in the centre of the wall. Apply the paint.

2 Place the swan stencil A at the same level on the left-hand side of the scallop and apply the paint. Clean the stencil by wiping with a small amount of white spirit on a cloth. Dry thoroughly. Reverse stencil A and stencil on the right-hand side of the scallop. Repeat the design to fit the space available.

3 Mask off one row of stencil B and use it to apply a top border approximately 2.5 cm (1 in) above the scallop design. Repeat the reverse design for a bottom border.

PROJECT PATTERN

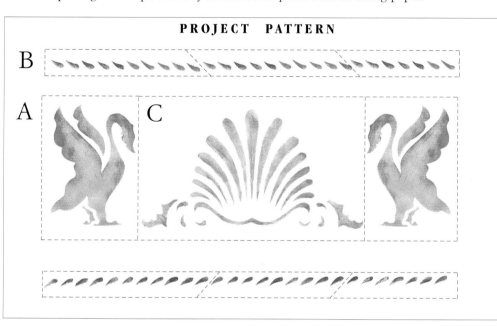

B

A   C

PREPARING THE COLOURS
Rub a small amount of jade onto a palette, and a separate amount of white, then blend together equal amounts of white and jade to create a tint. Blend a further amount of three-quarters white and one-quarter tint to create a hint of jade colour.

APPLYING THE COLOURS
Apply the hint of jade colour all over the stencil. Then, starting at the bottom of the stencil, stipple and blend in the neat jade, changing to the pale jade, gradually working upwards and outwards towards the outside edges of the stencil. Fade out the colours gradually to leave the lighter shade at the tips of the edges.

CREATING PATTERNED WALLPAPER
Carefully measure the wall to space your pattern at equal distances, using a plumbline or chalkline, and mark the wall with chalk. Measure from the top of the wall to the bottom and divide it equally so that the pattern fits. A dark shade of stencil colour is very effective on a pale wall and vice versa.

REGAL SWANS & SCALLOPS VARIATIONS

Although very easy to stencil, these designs appear intricate and sophisticated when painted and colours such as Prussian blue and Viridian will result in a dramatic colour mood. Use special ceramic paint to transform plain tiles in a bathroom or simply paint a border stencil above the tiles in a colour that matches or complements your bathroom suite.

TEARDROP PATTERN (STENCIL B)

SWANS BORDER (STENCIL A)

SWANS AND SCALLOPS BORDER (STENCILS A AND C)

TEARDROP STRIPES (STENCIL B)

SCALLOP MOTIFS (STENCIL C)

PAIRS OF SWANS BORDER (STENCIL A)

SCALLOPS EDGING (STENCIL C)

SWANS AND SCALLOP (STENCILS A AND C)

SWANS, SCALLOP AND TEARDROP (STENCILS A, B AND C)

DOUBLE TEARDROP BORDER (STENCIL B)

SCALLOPS AND SWIRLS BORDER (STENCIL C)

SCALLOPS BORDER (STENCIL C)

FLEUR-DE-LYS WITH SCROLLS

The fleur-de-lys was inspired by the majestic lily flower and has been widely used since the twelfth century. It is a very stylish design to use for a traditional border to a room, on flooring, on fabrics and for numerous other uses. It can enhance decorative boxes and be used to create wonderful wrapping paper and greetings cards. The fleur-de-lys combines well with traditional scroll patterns in deep earth colours and bronze. Deep red and gilt are opulent colours for cushions and curtain fabrics teamed with gold trimmings and accessories.

PAINT COLOUR GUIDE

Coffee   Chestnut brown   Bronze powder

MAKING THE BORDER PATTERN

1 Mark out a horizontal line on the wall, then place the fleur-de-lys stencil C in the centre, apply the paint and remove the stencil. Fixing spray can be applied to prevent smudging.

2 Draw a chalk guideline from the centre of the fleur-de-lys pattern so that it extends to each side.

3 Take stencils A and B. Make sure they are both mirror images, with the smaller ends of the scrolls nearest the centre. Align the smaller ends of the scrolls with the centre of the fleur-de-lys pattern, placing them at each side on the chalkline.

4 Then, using scroll stencils A and B again, place the larger scroll ends together (allow 1 cm [1/2 in] space between) and stencil one more scroll at each side. Position stencil D at the space between the top of the two large scrolls and apply paint. Repeat to complete.

PROJECT PATTERN

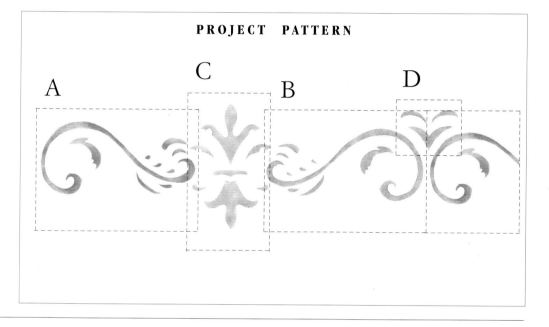

A   C   B   D

APPLYING THE COLOURS

Use rich earth colour oil sticks in chestnut and coffee brown, keeping the two colours separate on the palette. Paint on the lighter colour, then immediately randomly stipple the darker colour on top to give depth and contrast. The medium remains sticky and is the perfect base on which to apply bronze powder. Do not remove the stencil at this stage.

HIGHLIGHTING WITH BRONZE

Leaving the stencil in place (to contain the powder within specific areas), dip an art brush into the jar of bronze powder. Then, holding your hand underneath and the brush approximately 15 cm (6 in) away from the stencil, gently blow the powder off the brush into the paint. This creates a wonderful burnished effect.

FABRIC PAINT

When applying specialized fabric paint it is essential to position the fabric so that it is taut, and to place blotting paper behind the cloth. Fix the stencil with spray adhesive and apply the paint with a gentle swirling technique. Place a clean cotton cloth on top of the design and seal with a medium-heat iron.

FLEUR-DE-LYS WITH SCROLLS VARIATIONS

These designs can be used to give the illusion of heraldic emblems in the form of feathers, scrolls and arrows. They can be stencilled singly or rearranged in a variety of ways. Try stencilling them onto cushions and curtains made of shot taffetas, silks and brocades using dazzling metallic paint.

SCROLLS (STENCILS A AND B)

SMALL LILY PATTERN (STENCIL D)

SCROLLS AND FLEUR-DE-LYS (STENCILS A, B AND C)

LEFT: FLEUR-DE-LYS PATTERN (STENCIL C)

RIGHT: SMALL LILY REPEAT (STENCIL D)

SCROLL BORDER (STENCIL A)

FLEUR-DE-LYS EDGING (STENCIL C)

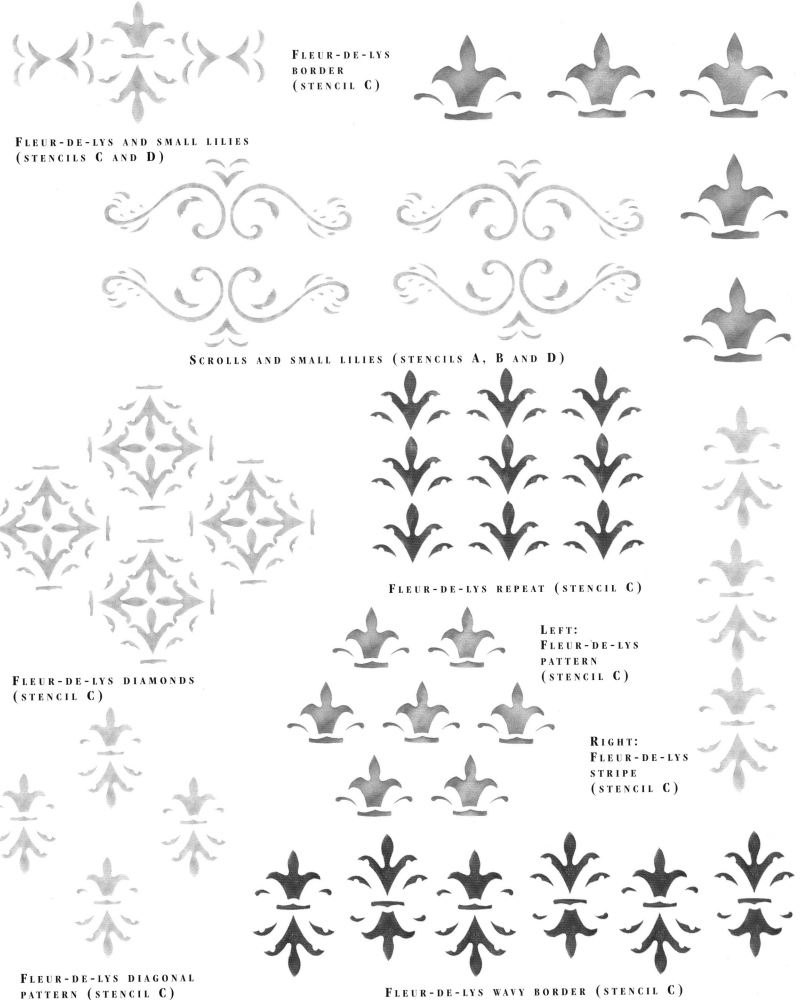

FLEUR-DE-LYS BORDER (STENCIL C)

FLEUR-DE-LYS AND SMALL LILIES (STENCILS C AND D)

SCROLLS AND SMALL LILIES (STENCILS A, B AND D)

FLEUR-DE-LYS DIAMONDS (STENCIL C)

FLEUR-DE-LYS REPEAT (STENCIL C)

LEFT: FLEUR-DE-LYS PATTERN (STENCIL C)

RIGHT: FLEUR-DE-LYS STRIPE (STENCIL C)

FLEUR-DE-LYS DIAGONAL PATTERN (STENCIL C)

FLEUR-DE-LYS WAVY BORDER (STENCIL C)

ROMAN EMPEROR & COLUMNS

With the use of bold black on white, this Roman head, classic column and plinth design can create a dramatic look. When the colours are reversed white on black the effect is equally stunning. The designs look good teamed with wrought-iron lights, candlesticks and curtain poles and, if stencilled onto white cotton fabric, you can make inexpensive matching curtains or blinds.

The column can be extended to any length and then the plinth added, and the rope design can be similarly adapted and also used as framing.

PAINT COLOUR GUIDE

Black   White

CREATING A MURAL

1 Find the centre vertical line of the mural area and position stencils B and D. Mark the length of the rope to the required size.

2 Position the head stencil A at each side of the rope, allowing adequate space to create a frame around each head. The heads need to be mirrored on opposite sides. Mark out the area with chalk.

3 Position the columns (stencil C), add the capitals (stencil E) and plinths (stencil F) and mark out with chalk. Once the complete mural has been planned you can stencil it in following your chalk guidelines.

PROJECT PATTERN

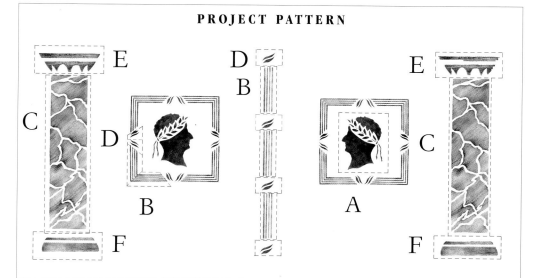

DRY-BRUSHING

The technique of dry-brushing the black paint onto the stencil will give a textured effect rather than a solid black matt finish. Lightly dip the tip of the brush into the paint and wipe off the excess on a cloth. Then brush on quickly in different directions rather than stippling, to create a lined effect.

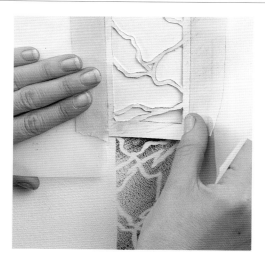

EXTENDING THE COLUMNS

Your wall mural layout will depend on the area you wish to decorate. Use spray adhesive to fix the plinth stencil F in position for the bottom of the column, then position stencil C 1 cm (¹/₂ in) directly above the plinth and apply the black paint to both stencils using the dry-brushing technique. To lengthen the column repeat stencil C directly on top of the previous one. Place capital stencil E in position 1 cm (¹/₂ in) above the column.

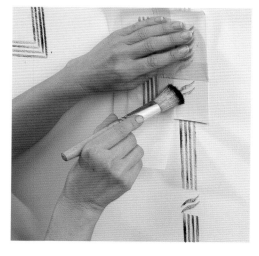

CREATING THE ROPE EFFECT

Use stencil B as your basic rope, either as a border or for a vertical rope as shown opposite. Overlay stencil D at each end of the straight rope. Repeat as many times as you require.

ROMAN EMPEROR & COLUMNS VARIATIONS

Just see how effective and dramatic these designs look in black or white. Framed silhouette pictures can be stencilled onto a wall by combining the head and straight rope stencils, or you can stencil onto paper for a picture in a real frame, or directly onto glass. Rich Roman interiors featured extravagant purple and gold, so try using these as alternative colours for borders and head laurels.

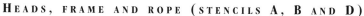

HEADS, FRAME AND ROPE (STENCILS A, B AND D)

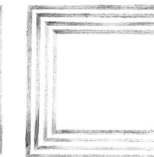

FRAMES (STENCIL B)

FRAMED HEADS (STENCILS A, B AND D)

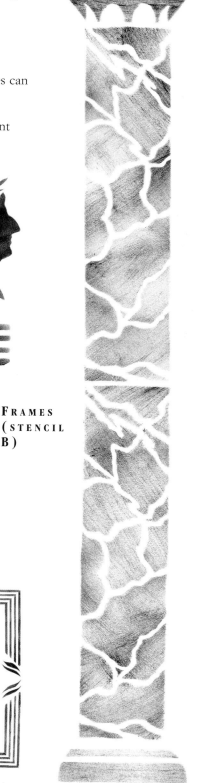

COLUMN (STENCILS C, E AND F)

ROPE BORDER (STENCIL D)

FRAME AND ROPE CORNER
(STENCILS B AND D)

COLUMNS AND ROPE (STENCILS C, D, E AND F)

ROPE (STENCIL D)

HEADS BORDER (STENCIL A)

CAPITALS AND COLUMNS BORDER (STENCILS B AND E)

SUPPLIERS

Crown Decorative Products
PO Box 37, Crown House
Hollins Road, Darwen
Lancashire (Tel. 01254 704951)

A. S. Handover
37 Mildmay Grove
London N1 4RH (Tel. 0171 359 4696)

Plasti-kote Limited
London Road Industrial Estate
Sawston
Cambridge CB2 4TR
(Tel. 01223 836400)

Stencil Store Company Ltd
20/21 Heronsgate Road
Chorleywood
Hertfordshire WD3 5BN
(Tel.01923 285577/88)

ACKNOWLEDGEMENTS

Merehurst Limited wish to thank the following for their help: The Water Monopoly; Decorative Living; Damask; Nice Irma's; Borovick Fabric; Cath Kidston Ltd; Cologne & Cotton; McKinney & Co.

First published in 1997 by Merehurst Limited
Ferry House, 51–57 Lacy Road, Putney, London SW15 1PR

© Copyright 1997 Merehurst Limited
Reprinted in 1999
ISBN 1-85391-696-X

A catalogue record of this book is available from the British Library.

Edited by Geraldine Christy
Photography by Graeme Ainscough
Styling by Clare Louise Hunt

Colour separation by Bright Arts (HK) Limited
Printed in Singapore

Julie Collins is one of the UK's most versatile specialist decorators and she makes regular TV appearances to demonstrate her skills and ideas. 'Creative Day' courses are available with Julie Collins, covering stencilling, paint techniques and transforming old and new furniture. For further information telephone 0181 343 2651.